THE MILLIONAIRE AUDITOR

THINK LIKE A
MILLIONAIRE
AUDITOR

How To Build Practical Efficiency, Increase Revenue and Experience Peace of Mind That Will Transform Your Business, Leadership & Life

---

Special _FREE_ Bonus Gift for You
To help you to achieve more success, there are
FREE BONUS RESOURCES for you at:
www.FreeGiftFromCoachMichael.com

- Cutting-edge training video on how top achievers attract more career opportunities, magnetize recruiters and create more sought-after skills
- Downloadable IT audit request template called: "Get Relevant Audit Data Now"

MICHAEL J. HARRISON

Copyright © 2022 Harrison Cyber Security Intelligence Inc.

ALL RIGHTS RESERVED. No part of this book or its associated ancillary materials may be reproduced or transmitted in any form or by any means, electronic or mechanical, including photocopying, recording, or by any informational storage or retrieval system without permission from the publisher.

PUBLISHED BY: Harrison Cyber Security Intelligence Inc.,

DISCLAIMER AND/OR LEGAL NOTICES

While all attempts have been made to verify information provided in this book and its ancillary materials, neither the author or publisher assumes any responsibility for errors, inaccuracies or omissions and is not responsible for any financial loss by customer in any manner. Any slights of people or organizations are unintentional. If advice concerning legal, financial, accounting or related matters is needed, the services of a qualified professional should be sought. This book and its associated ancillary materials, including verbal and written training, is not intended for use as a source of legal, financial or accounting advice. You should be aware of the various laws governing business transactions or other business practices in your particular geographical location.

EARNINGS & INCOME DISCLAIMER

With respect to the reliability, accuracy, timeliness, usefulness, adequacy, completeness, and/ or suitability of information provided in this book, Michael J. Harrison, Harrison Cyber Security Intelligence Inc., its partners, associates, affiliates, consultants, and/or presenters make no warranties, guarantees, representations, or claims of any kind. Readers' results will vary depending on a number of factors. Any and all claims or representations as to income earnings are not to be considered as average earnings. Testimonials are not representative. This book and all products and services are for educational and informational purposes only. Use caution and see the advice of qualified professionals. Check with your accountant, attorney or professional advisor before acting on this or any information. You agree that Michael J. Harrison and/or Harrison Cyber Security Intelligence Inc. is not responsible for the success or failure of your personal, business, health or financial decisions relating to any information presented by Michael J. Harrison, Harrison Cyber Security Intelligence Inc., or company products/services. Earnings potential is entirely dependent on the efforts, skills and application of the individual person. Any examples, stories, references, or case studies are for illustrative purposes only and should not be interpreted as testimonies and/or examples of what reader and/or consumers can generally expect from the information. No representation in any part of this information, materials and/or seminar training are guarantees or promises for actual performance. Any statements, strategies, concepts, techniques, exercises and ideas in the information, materials and/or seminar training offered are simply opinion or experience, and thus should not be misinterpreted as promises, typical results or guarantees (expressed or implied). The author and publisher (Michael J. Harrison, Harrison Cyber Security Intelligence Inc. (Harrintel) or any of Harrintel's representatives) shall in no way, under any circumstances, be held liable to any party (or third party) for any direct, indirect, punitive, special, incidental or other consequential damages arising directly or indirectly from any use of books, materials and or seminar trainings, which is provided "as is," and without warranties.

PRINTED IN CANADA

WHAT OTHERS ARE SAYING ABOUT MICHAEL J. HARRISON & HIS STRATEGIES

"Michael J. Harrison's ways of thinking have the power to inspire people!"

-**James Malinchak**, featured on ABC's Hit TV Show, "Secret Millionaire" (viewed by 50 million+ worldwide), Bestselling author of *Millionaire Success Secrets*, founder, www.BigMoneySpeaker.com

"Ahh! Well thanks so much for having me Michael. You're such a pleasure to work with…"

-**Kim Walsh Phillips**, founder of Powerful Professionals, Bestselling author of *No B.S. Guide To Direct Response Social Media Marketing*

"Thank you for what you're doing. Blessings and bravo to the work that you're doing. If we all ignite each other and upraise humanity, we are going to have an amazing incredible place to be, to live, to grow and to welcome in the next generation. So thank you for the work you're doing…"

-**Lady JB Owen**, founder and CEO of Ignite Publishing, Ignite Moments Media, JBO Global Inc. and Lotus Liners

"Awesome! Beautiful! Well God bless you!"

-**Luz Delia Gerber**, CEO & Co-Founder of Michael E. Gerber Companies, Author of *Oh, My Body!*

"Thanks Michael! I appreciate it and thank you for doing this."

-**Aigné Goldsby, Esq.**, founder of Black Esquire

"Michael J. Harrison is very knowledgeable and skilled at his craft. He is very dependable, resourceful and easy to talk with."

-**Nicole Patterson-Gilbert**, President and co-founder of Zudeti Consulting Inc.

"Michael's relentless effort to achieve his dreams every day is super impressive!"

-**Funmilayo Kazim,** MBA, CISA, CISM, Technology Risk Auditor

"Sir Mike…I have always admired your attitude and professionalism, and this will certainly take you a far way."

-**Carolyn Bell Wisdom,** CISA

"…I didn't really know much of this information. It is obvious that he [Michael] has a great understanding of his profession."

-**Angela Heath**, President of TKC Incorporated

"Michael's ideas have the power to change lives..."

-**Deloris Penny Johnson,** Restoration Outreach Ministries

"Michael explains his strategies in simple terms. As someone who is not business minded, I feel these concepts will help me succeed."

-**Kimberly Taylor Mullin**

"… the author's gentle tone and patience helped me understand some key points!"

-**Marcia L. Haynes-Cody,** RN

"As a board director, understanding the importance of technology from a Cyber Security point of view is crucial to carrying out your duty of oversight...I am eternally grateful to Michael for taking the time to provide this thoughtful and concise information for those of us who are not born in the digital age."

-**Valerie Romanow**, Director

MOTIVATE AND INSPIRE OTHERS!

"Share This Book"

Retail $24.95

Special Quantity Discounts

5-20 Books	$21.95
21-99 Books	$18.95
100-499 Books	$15.95
500-999 Books	$10.95
1,000+ Books	$8.95

To Place an Order Contact:

info@MichaelHarrisonJM.com
www.MichaelHarrisonJM.com
www.MorningSuccessPlan.com

THE IDEAL PROFESSIONAL SPEAKER FOR YOUR NEXT EVENT!

Any organization that wants to develop their people to become "extraordinary," needs to hire Michael for a keynote and/or workshop training!

TO CONTACT OR BOOK MICHAEL TO SPEAK:

Harrison Cyber Security Intelligence Inc.

info@MichaelHarrisonJM.com
www.MichaelHarrisonJM.com
www.MorningSuccessPlan.com

THE IDEAL COACH FOR YOU!

If you're ready to overcome challenges, have major breakthroughs and achieve higher levels, then you will love having Michael as your coach!

TO CONTACT OR BOOK MICHAEL TO SPEAK:

Harrison Cyber Security Intelligence Inc.

info@MichaelHarrisonJM.com
www.MichaelHarrisonJM.com
www.MorningSuccessPlan.com

DEDICATION

It is with respect, admiration and sincere appreciation, that I dedicate this book to my wonderful family.

Without you and the lessons you taught me throughout my life, I would not have the blessing of being where I am today.

Thank you from the bottom of my heart!

I love you dearly!

TABLE OF CONTENTS

Introduction: A Message to You! 14
1. Where It All Began 18
2. It's Your Business 24
3. The UPCO Blueprint 27
4. User Access Management 29
    User access granting 30
    Shared user IDs 32
    The fantastic four controls 33
    User access termination 34
    Access rights review 36
    Monitoring activities of privileged users 38
5. Password and Configuration Management 41
    Information Security Policy and Password Standard 42
    Password Composition 43
6. *Program* Change Management 51
    Test plans 53
    The developer, tester and implementer 54
    Emergency changes 56
    Post-implementation review 57
7. Computer Operations 59
    Data backup configuration 62
    Data restoration 63
    Configuration change monitoring 64

Vulnerability assessment and penetration testing 64

8. Unlock the Secrets 66

SECRET 1: Create a secure storage location 71

SECRET 2: Generate your user listings 73

SECRET 3: Perform and document your access rights review 75

SECRET 4: Update your information security policy and password standard 77

SECRET 5: Document, document, document 79

BONUS SECRET 1: Capture the date and time 85

BONUS SECRET 2: Build rapport with your stakeholders 87

Bringing It All Together 88

The Reward 94

ONE LAST MESSAGE 95

ACKNOWLEDGEMENTS 96

ADDITIONAL RESOURCES 98

A MESSAGE TO YOU!

You may not know this, but once upon a time, on a bright and sunny January afternoon a few years ago, I and my family packed our suitcases to go to a foreign land.

We packed everything we needed in there and came to this wonderful country called Canada. Now when we boarded the plane, we had every bit of courage that things would work out but when the airport doors opened, it was a different sight that January night.

It looked like there was snow everywhere and this was the very first time we were seeing snow. And the temperature was -40 degrees cold.

What this means for you is this.

Like all conditions in life, you can plan but God must give approval. Situations will work out for you in the most amazing way and you get to enjoy the opportunities that exist within each challenge. The opportunity to rise higher above your situation and gain the necessary skills to follow through to success.

Being in this wonderful place is beneficial and I get to positively impact your life by taking a chance on life. This is your gift and I am honored to be sharing my knowledge with you to transform your business, leadership and life.

My goal with this book is to ENCOURAGE you to act with INTEGRITY as a leader, to EMPOWER YOU to dream bigger and have PEACE OF MIND before, during and after any character-building situation.

Let me give you an example.

Whenever I am speaking for a faith-based group, a youth group, addressing business executives in the boardroom, whether it's an association, a non-profit, a university, consulting for a project or just giving life-changing advice. Whenever I am speaking for any of these groups, one thing is for certain, you must be knowledgeable about the topic you are speaking about so that you can transform lives.

You will discover strategies and secrets to breakthrough an impossible situation into one that benefits all parties involved. You will have the knowledge that is required to produce your desired result.

I am blessed to learn from many mentors throughout my lifetime. It is my honor to meet you through the pages of this book and to share that wisdom with you.

I believe that every human being with the right knowledge of a particular topic, can transform their lives, leadership and business. And by doing so, can transform the lives of others. That is what I want for you throughout the pages of this book.

Thank you for reading and when you are finished, please share this book with your friends and family so that you can help them experience peace of mind that will transform their business, leadership and life.

Is integrity, trust and leading by example your way of life?

Rise to the next level of your leadership potential.

Are you committed to an investment in yourself that yields premium benefits?

Join Master Mind with Mike https://bit.ly/3eCgPh5

SAVE on your investment https://bit.ly/3Jkewhw

1

Where It All Began

"Take ownership to gain mastery."
~Erwin McManus

Let me tell you about when I was an information systems auditor. It all began in university where I selected the elective to diversify my Computer Science degree. I was curious about the Information Technology (IT) auditing elective and the history of events were fascinating. Upon completion of the degree program, I finally made entry into the elite big 4 firm that helped to hone my skills, so that I could effectively advice decision-makers.

Being a trusted advisor performing a fiduciary role and carrying out information system audit assignments, I was privileged to conduct numerous client interviews at the board level to the operations manager, in Jamaica, Canada and USA.

At first, this can be intimidating, especially if this is a new client and/or if you are the only one assigned to the project. However, when you are a part of a prestigious group of professionals who are highly respected for the insights you bring, confidence in yourself is restored.

What this means for you is this.

You are benefiting from my years of collaborating with several international clients in various industries. From big four firms, insurance companies, universities, banking sector, technology sector, oil and gas sector, logistics sector, a bus manufacturing company to even the Government of Manitoba.

You are benefiting from my unique and mutual relationship with PwC through former service delivery to their clients. In addition, the knowledge obtained while assisting those wonderful clients to design appropriate IT controls that support financial reporting, ensured that their controls were operating in an effective manner to reduce misstatements.

Now it is your turn to be free from worrisome audits and thrive in business, leadership and life.

How would you like to reduce your IT audit cost?

You may feel like every year you pay SO much, but **your business income increases so slightly that you can't justify paying for this service.**

Every time the auditors come; **you may feel like they are asking for so much more information than prior years.**

You may even feel like reducing your audit cost is a **mystery you will never figure out.**

Well, what if I told you…

By preparing well for the audit and applying these secrets and strategies…

You can *build practical efficiency* into your audit process, *increase revenue* and experience *peace of mind.*

It's simple!

You would not have to pay more for the time delays in getting the right audit evidence to your auditors.

No more back and forth communications to obtain the appropriate audit evidence that supports audit control testing. Your business is about to rise to a new level with the formula being shared in the remaining pages.

Are you ready to discover these strategies, secrets plus additional bonus secrets toward your audit cost breakthrough and peace of mind?

Great! Let's get started.

"Day by day, in every way, I am getting better and better…" - Emil Coué.

What is the single biggest challenge you are trying to solve in your business?

Share your comments and/or feedback at https://bit.ly/3Hm6MKB

2

It's Your Business

"Be honest about your current reality."
~Michael Hyatt

Financial reporting in the next decade relies on information systems (IS) to compete with other businesses, including yours.

Businesses with a significant amount of revenue and/or are listed on some securities exchange, often employ the services of information systems auditors to evaluate the appropriate design and operating effectiveness of IS controls to reduce Information Technology (IT) risks to an acceptable level for management.

These IS controls are established by management and are expected to be operating effectively to reduce the risk of using IT in your businesses so that you can increase efficiency, increase revenue, reduce cost and time.

Having healthy financial statements from financial reporting helps investors and shareholders make informed decisions about the financial health of your business. Therefore, the controls in your IT environment or the lack thereof, impacts the information coming from those information systems associated with financial reporting.

At times, organizations receive an unqualified audit opinion and later are victims of cyber breaches. In this book, you will discover the basics of an IT audit that supports financial reporting so that you can enjoy peace of mind.

So, over the remaining pages of this book, I am going to give you so much value that I trust you will see it and apply it to your audit experience in your business.

Before I go any further, I have a question for you.

Are you ready and committed to transforming your business?

Well, let's go!

Up, up and transform!

3

The UPCO Blueprint

"Make success a natural part of your business."
~Jay Abraham

Now I want to cover our four-step blueprint to help 100,000 business leaders globally who are ready to design effective Information Technology (IT) controls that support financial reporting so that you can reduce your risk of cyber breaches.

There are so many cyber-attacks out there right now and it is my belief that once you have appropriately designed IT controls, that you have done the foundational work needed to reduce your risk of cyber breaches.

"So Michael, why did you come up with your four-step blueprint?", you may ask.

You may be a business leader who is confused about the need for an audit, and I wanted to make the requirements in the audit process easier for you. The blueprint came about because of working with many corporate companies over the years that I have dialed it down to these four steps.

It is like you're effortlessly going up a step. So, here's an easy way to remember the phrase,

Users Pass Change Ops

These are the four steps that you will discover today, and each step has different dimensions to them that is guaranteed to increase your awareness of them.

My big promise to you is that by sharing the four-step blueprint, you will reduce your IT risk in financial reporting to an acceptable level. You will also enhance your IT audit experience so that you can have a high level of peace of mind and revenue in your business.

4

User Access Management

"Have ethics in business. No matter what, do not compromise your integrity."
~Molly Bloom

Step one in our four-step blueprint

It was summertime and I was so excited to work at the amusement park in Sandusky, Ohio. So many rides to choose from, especially the dragster rollercoaster that sped 0 to 60 miles per hour in seconds.

The lights cycle down from orange, yellow to green and it shot down the track and suddenly turned vertically upwards and down the other side. Wow, what a rush of energy. I was so excited because I had my tamperproof all access wrist band which granted me to…you guessed it, all the rides in the park.

There were many access levels for park attendees, park employees and suppliers entering through the security gate.

What this means for you is this.

You get to review all the user accounts on systems in your enterprise and know who can do what, whether they are authorized or not.

User access granting

Obtaining a list of new users in your organization from an Human Resources (HR) report for testing the operational effectiveness of a control, is a last resort.

The application users have accounts that were created on it in whatever period that is being tested. Therefore, obtaining a list of users from the application is preferred.

But suppose there is no created date logged in the application to indicate when a user account was created. Then reliance can be placed on the HR listing which is cross-referenced with the listing from the application to establish the user accounts that were created within a particular period. The application user listing can then serve as a benchmark for subsequent comparisons in future years.

The new accesses on the application should be supported by a request and an authorized approval from management.

The approval must not be granted after the user account is provisioned because this will result in an audit finding. The user access level requested should be the same level or less than what was granted.

If excess access was granted, it should be supported by an additional authorized approval for the additional access that was granted. Otherwise, an audit finding may result.

Operating systems (OSes) and databases usually log a created entry for new accounts, and it becomes easy to identify user accounts created in a particular period.

A mechanism should be implemented to let the owner of the user account know the initial logon credentials and be required to change that password on the first log on attempt. Additionally, the requester of the user access should have some means of knowing that the request has been processed.

Shared user IDs

Sometimes user IDs are shared between two or more persons or groups of persons. This practice should be restricted as much as possible because accountability will be difficult to establish. However, where this practice cannot be avoided, the use of those shared user IDs should be documented.

The users who use the shared ID at a particular time of day should be logged. As a control, this shared ID should be the responsibility of a manager and users should be required to request use of this shared ID. A check-in, checkout process could be implemented for this. There is software on the marketplace designed to securely store, check-in and check-out shared IDs.

The fantastic four controls

There are four controls that you should have in your organization. You have employees who are users, whether they have the title of CEO or an intern and each has a user account.

To make it really simple:

1. When users are added to the applications and/or systems,
2. Procedures that you follow when users are deactivated.
3. Procedures that you follow when user access rights need to be reviewed
4. Activities of privileged users that need to be reviewed

Now the first control.

In granting access to your application or to your system, there needs to be some way of communicating this user access request to the persons involved. Most likely, your IT department does the creation of the user accounts by receiving an email request or a form that is submitted by a department manager. In recent times, an electronic form is more likely to be submitted.

One thing to be clear, is that all requests for a user account creation must have management approval.

For every new user ID that is on a particular application and/or system, one thing to note is that whatever permission was requested on the user access form for that user, it should be the permission or the access rights that are applied to that user account.

The next thing is that management approval should be received before the account is set up in the application and/or system. If you as a business leader have these in place, then more than likely you will pass the access granting control.

User access termination

In the case of voluntary employee departure, user access termination should be configured at the network level for the predetermined date, which is within 24 hours. Physical security access termination should complement the logical access termination. One problem that may arise is the communication gap between HR and IT.

This is operational in nature and if unresolved for a long time, may result in a cyber incident for the active accounts of terminated employees.

Accountability for unauthorized activities may be difficult to establish since the terminated employee is no longer on the payroll.

Once network level access is deactivated within 24 hours, downstream systems could be deactivated within 5 business days. This of course should be documented in the information security policy that governs the user access termination process.

When users are removed, there are some controls or some mechanism that you need to be in place so that requested users are removed in a reasonable time frame. Removal of access should be within 24 hours at both physical and logical levels, which is a good time interval.

Nowadays, most organizations use a directory service such as Active Directory (AD) where if an employee is being terminated, their access can be pre-configured in the network to automatically remove access for that account.

Access granting and termination controls are preventive controls that if there is a deficiency in any one can be detected by the periodic review of the access rights of users within the applications and/or systems.

Access rights review

At a predetermined date during the financial year, the application owner of the application should request a listing of users and their associated access rights within their application. The application owner should be knowledgeable of each access right and the function it performs. The application owner should verify the completeness of the user listing provided, before the revalidation process begins.

A defined time frame should be established in which the revalidation process is completed. This also should be defined in the information security policy. Upon completion of the access rights validation, continued access, modification of access or access removal should be indicated in order for it to be processed in a timely manner.

This detective control, when performed multiple times per year, will be effective in detecting unauthorized access granting or missed termination requests.

The revalidation exercise should be done in a timely manner so that it does not flow over to the following financial year.

For example, if the permissions need to be adjusted or removed, then it should be done within the time frame of the year so that whatever action needs to be performed, is done.

If user access needs to be removed because they are no longer doing that particular task requiring that information, the access rights review serves as a catch-all control. Additionally, if something is missed during the termination phase or the access granting phase, this serves as a catch-all to any of those missed access requests.

Let me give you an example of this process.

So, one control that you need to have in place is that the application owners need to request the user listing from the applications and/or systems that they are responsible for in order to have the revalidation process done.

It is important to note that there is a way for the application owner to verify the accuracy and completeness of the user listing provided to them.

It cannot be that the application owner is totally dependent on the IT personnel to just give them the listing and get the stamp of approval because it's coming from IT. Therefore, the information that is provided is to be accurate and complete because your auditor will not appreciate it otherwise.

So, there should be a way that the application owner knows that the user list that is provided is accurate and complete.

One solution is that the application owner could ask the IT personnel to provide the script or the context in which the information was retrieved from the system, and they walk through it to see if what has been performed is reasonable.

Monitoring activities of privileged users

Now how about the privileged users?

I mean those users who have more than the normal access within your applications and within your operating systems or databases.

Privileged users supporting the information systems that impact financial reporting, have powerful access privileges that are often overlooked.

These users are trusted employees that management has delegated as data custodians. However, their activities must be within normal business use of such privileges. Therefore, management should establish a review control in key systems and sensitive tasks to periodically check for compliance to their job function.

Triggers should be set up on sensitive processes, critical database tables or records to ensure that these users are doing whatever is within their job duties. You should be aware that there can be a lot of activity alerts that will be sent out once this is set up. However, just be mindful of what is critical to your business when you set these up.

Setting them up is not the final step, there needs to be a regular review of those activities to ensure that there are no unauthorized users doing anything that they are not supposed to do. The review process is the control, so if it is not reviewed, you do not have a control.

The functionality of a security information and event management (SIEM) tool could be a good investment to help with doing the review of privileged user access activities. These alerts should be investigated for unauthorized activities and documented for management review. Implementing a security orchestration, automation and reporting (SOAR) tool is also a very good investment in this regard.

So, do you find the information valuable so far?

Great!

Your next step…

Want your employees looking out for the longevity of your enterprise without the long hours of computer training?

Get access to the Security Awareness Design Program at

https://bit.ly/3tXBYux

Let's carry on!

5

Password and Configuration Management

"You attract people with your confidence."
~Gloria Mayfield Banks

Step two in our four-step blueprint

A few years ago, in the news, the computer systems of a popular airline were hacked, and I wondered, how interesting! Companies like these should have their systems well protected from breaches like these. However, that was not the case. Being in established for a few years, the investment in the computer systems of the day was may have been significant. So, it would be a costly upgrade which the airline's management was not prepared to pay.

After a few years, I had the opportunity to review the password controls of this airline and the systems at the time couldn't support complex passwords.

What this means for you is this.

You now can look in your current IT environment to see where you may be vulnerable.

Information Security Policy and Password Standard

An information security policy is the starting point of any effective control in businesses today. From the policy will flow the password standard which dictates the password parameters to be configured on applications, operating systems, databases and networks in your IT environment.

Oftentimes, an information security policy is non-existent, therefore a password standard cannot be developed. Where a policy document exists that resembles the contents of a password standard, it may not be up to date on industry best practices.

A policy is established by senior management and is high-level in nature. It outlines statements such as ... *a strong password should be used on systems where technically feasible. Where it is not technically feasible, compensating controls should be implemented in those systems or the processes that depend on those systems.*

Password Composition

The password should be of sufficient length to meet industry best practices. Passphrases should be used to ensure sufficient password length is achieved.

Password complexity should be used to make it difficult to break by unauthorized persons.

User accounts should be allowed a finite number of attempts to enter a password or passphrase. The user account should be locked until it is unlocked by an administrator and the number of login attempts should be reset after a finite time.

Users of systems should be able to keep their changed password for a minimum of at least one day and a maximum of 90 days.

Now the password standard outlines the specific settings that must be configured across applications, operating systems, databases and network devices. Where these settings are not documented in the password standard, it becomes difficult to assess the operating effectiveness of password controls.

Again, the information security policy should be approved by senior management and reviewed at least annually or when the activity will be conducted.

For the Microsoft Windows IT environment, Active Directory can be leveraged to enforce password settings on applications, OSes and sometimes databases such as Microsoft SQL Server. Sometimes organizations have been established for years and have made significant investments in technology which was the best at the time but are now legacy.

The legacy systems are often no longer supported by their vendors. Usually, the password standard is not applicable to these systems. One solution is to hide these systems behind a terminal service application such as Citrix, which is configured to use Active Directory credentials.

Compensating review control should be implemented to periodically review the Citrix logs for user activities that violate the use of another user's account, other than the owner of the Active Directory account.

When such an implementation is not practical to the business, senior management should document a waiver for the password weaknesses in those affected systems. Such waivers should be reviewed on an annual basis.

It is noteworthy that alphanumeric passwords are not equivalent to password complexity. For example, legacy mainframes that cannot enforce password complexity have alphanumeric passwords as the standard. Legacy mainframes are old technology, and not many professionals are knowledgeable about it and businesses often practice security by obscurity.

For these legacy systems, network segmentation is another technique/control that can be used where only authorized users and computers can access this resource.

Now here are four areas that you want to be aware of:

1. Single sign-on authentication
2. Direct application authentication
3. Legacy applications and accounts
4. Configuration change monitoring

There may be applications that use the network credentials to authenticate users. Such applications have a configuration screen that shows whether it is using the network credentials. This should be captured to support your audit evidence.

In order to look at single sign-on authentication, passwords must be composed in a certain way as previously mentioned. So, the minimum password length should be set up. Usually, eight characters or more.

The minimum password age which means how long a user needs to keep their password before they are allowed to change it. One day is usually appropriate.

The maximum password expiration which means how long the password is valid. An acceptable time frame is 90 days.

The password complexity which is any three of the four components or characteristics below:

1. An uppercase letter
2. A lowercase letter
3. A number or
4. A special character

Any three of those four.

You are aware that there are some applications that are not able to enforce this in their configuration.

So, what do you do about that?

Well, let's find out later on.

A companion to the password composition control is the account lockout policy and this goes hand in hand with the password policy. There are three areas to be aware of:

- The number of failed login attempts, usually three to four attempts
- The lockout duration and the best practice is that the account is locked until the administrator unlocks it
- The reset lockout counter usually 30 minutes

So once all of that is in place then you can look at single sign-on. It's like your passport into all the other applications and systems that use single sign on authentication.

One control to bear in mind is that in the configuration screen within the application where single sign-on is enabled, it needs to show that the application itself is using the network to authenticate the user.

This is something that the external auditor will look for when they are assessing whether the application is using single sign-on to authenticate users or not.

There are some applications, for example on the OS 400, where the application is integrated with the operating system. They do not use the single sign-on but rather they have their own authentication that needs to be entered once. Once you log into the application, the configuration screen of the password parameters needs to be set up in a way that it shows that the password parameters meet the password policy that is set up for the enterprise.

When it comes to legacy applications, it bears repeating here that these are those applications and systems that are no longer supported by the vendor and the password standard cannot be enforced. There are many applications and systems that I have seen over the years that fall into this category and some form of terminal server solution, for example Citrix, can be used to encapsulate these legacy applications.

This ensures that there is some form of control of who logs in to the legacy application. You can know from the logs of the terminal server solution, the user activity of whoever is logged on is really the right person that is logging on.

So, the review of those logs for user activity is critical. Therefore, if you as a business owner or leader is able to demonstrate that you have such a control in place, then you will pass this control.

So, are you comfortable not taking action?

Share your comments and/or feedback at https://bit.ly/3Hm6MKB

Okay let's move on.

6

Program Change Management

"The most powerful thing (you), a human being can do in life, is change your mind."

~Grant Cardone

Step three in our four-step blueprint

As the seasons change each year, I am fascinated by the beauty that each one brings. With my Nikon DSLR camera in hand, I set out in nature to visit flower gardens and capture the spring of new shoots as they stretch from their winter embrace.

Oh, look at the deer prancing across the road and disappears in the green canopy of the trees.

What this means for you is this.

Changes are everywhere and how you adjust to change, determines your experience.

Application programs are used by business leaders and their employees to carry out the business objectives of the organization. These application programs process transactions on a daily basis by authorized users with the necessary approval levels.

It is therefore important that changes to these application programs be done in an authorized and controlled manner. All such changes that will impact the functionality of the application should be requested by business users and/or technical support staff. These business users are more likely to make such requests, since they are using the applications daily.

When the requested application changes are deemed valid by management, development of the required changes can begin. Sometimes the developer of the change carries out functional tests. However, the testing of the developed changes should be done by the business users who initially requested the change.

Test plans

Test plans should be used to ensure that all functional areas are considered for testing and pre-existing components still operate as they should. The test results should be documented and reviewed by management to ensure the results are appropriate to meet the requested change.

Upon approval of the test results, a change advisory board (CAB) or equivalent, should approve the tested change to be migrated into the production environment. Preferably, applying the accepted version to the production environment can be done during a maintenance window when transaction processing is low to zero.

The developer, tester and implementer

The developer, tester and implementer should be different to ensure segregation of duties (SoD).

Where the developer is the implementer, a software could be used to perform the deployment into the production environment.

The requester at times can be the tester as well. You can think of it in the case of an end user of the application. For example, an application user may request a function in the application that is causing this issue or need this feature now. When everything is done, it is this request that will be tested to ensure that whatever was requested is what was developed by the developer.

So, in this case, the requester can be the tester.

Another thing to note, is that the developer must not be the final tester or the implementer because it is the end user who will be using the application. A scenario where this is not feasible is in the telecom industry where the implementer of the change is usually the developer and tester of that change.

Anyway, the end users need to be testing the developed changes. Separate personnel need to be implementing what has been developed.

But what if you have a small team?

What do you do?

Well, there could be another ID setup that is only released by management to the developer to implement whatever changes need to be implemented. The use of this ID should be documented somewhere, and the activities reviewed on a periodic basis. This will establish a control that you can rely on.

There should be end user testing and these testing should be documented, and management approve of the test results to ensure that the test results are according to what is in the test plans.

Another control that you should have in place is management approval of testing of the tested version. That means whatever was signed off on, management approval of that particular version should exist to ensure that is what gets into the production environment.

Emergency changes

Now what if there are emergencies that occur and of course, it happens. There are times when an emergency change to the functionality of an application is required. These emergency changes usually do not go through the normal change management process. After the emergency change is tested and implemented in the production environment, documentation and approval of the emergency change should be done.

There could be a special ID that is used for emergency purposes. Once there is documentation and management approval, then you have a control that you can rely upon.

There is also "after the fact" when everything in the enterprise is now stabilized. The documentation and approval of what was done needs to be in place so that when the external auditor comes in, you'll have that information ready at hand to furnish.

Rollback procedures should be included in all implemented application changes to ensure that if adverse conditions arise, the timeframe to return the business to a working state is greatly reduced.

Post-implementation review

Because there is a risk that changes can be introduced into the production environment and bypass the change management process, a mechanism should be in place to detect such changes.

Additionally, after the accepted change has been in production for a number of business cycles, an extraction of program files associated with the recently changed application should be taken and reviewed to ensure that all change objects have passed through the change management process. This review should be documented.

Most organizations fail the periodic review of post implementation of changes and now you are no longer one of them.

Again, how this should be done is that there is a review of the files or objects that are associated with the applications. In knowing the program files that were changed, you as an enterprise can capture those changes that did not pass through the change management process.

You should have the change advisory board (CAB) or equivalent review these changes to ensure that they actually went through the change management process. This is documented so that when the external auditor comes in, the information can be confidently provided to them.

7

Computer Operations

"Are you non-negotiable about your goals."
~Lisa Nichols

All right, the fourth step in our four-step blueprint

On leaving the elevator, we were laughing and chatting and greeted the receptionist with a hearty, "good morning, Allison!"

I entered the office and round the corner to my desk, I rested my backpack on the desk. As I took out my laptop and greeted my colleague sitting across from me, the red light on the desk phone yelled for my attention.

So, I entered the password and listened to the first voicemail message. It was one of my clients I audited a few months earlier. They had gotten their IT audit findings report which highlighted what the management needed to act upon.

So, as I listened, my heart sank within me. It was about 7 a.m. and it was the cry for help. Their systems were inaccessible. They were hacked!

A significant amount of data was wiped clean. Operations ground to a halt and management was scrambling for solutions. Fortunately, they had a working backup of their data and restored operations within a few days.

What this means for you is this.

If you connect to the Internet, you are vulnerable but that is a business risk. So, secure your business systems appropriately.

All enterprises have computer operations and there are some critical controls that once you have them in place, can help you to reduce IT risks.

As applications process business transactions on a daily basis, there are times when errors occur. Applications should be configured to flag errors and log an incident in the management software for further investigation. That's critical because if your application does not tell you when something is wrong and you have to depend on the users to tell you, you may be losing business right there.

Upon investigation, the errors should be prioritized and processed according to the incident management policy. When you configure the application to alert on errors, the ability to change these flags should be restricted to authorized persons so that when these incidents occur, you will know as an enterprise. Also, that none of the incidents would be suppressed by any person with the privilege to change those. These application flags should be restricted from unauthorized changes.

Again, all incidents or errors should be documented in your incident management software. That way, you have a central repository where all this information can be analyzed over time to see the trends that are occurring in the enterprise and management is able to look into these trends to understand what is happening.

Is there a root cause for these number of incidents? Yes!

Most organizations have a service level agreement (SLA) where they categorize each incident whether priority 1, priority 2, priority 3 or 4 and there is a defined time frame in which each priority type incident is resolved.

That is usually documented or is a part of the incident management policy.

Now you may say, "what about the cyber incident policy?"

This can be a subset of the incident management policy and addressed in a similar way.

Data backup configuration

Business transaction data should be backed up based on the data backup and data classification policy. So, if the applications are critical to your business, the data backup frequency and schemes must be configured accordingly.

You want to ensure that when it comes to your backups, configuring for daily, weekly or quarterly schemes is perfectly fine.

Whatever is configured in the backup software, should reflect what is actually taking place in the operations of the business. If there is a failure in any of these backup sequences, then there should be some mechanism to have it re-run the next day.

Data restoration

The most important criteria in having an organization or an enterprise recover is that the backups are able to be restored in a timely manner.

There should be regular restoration tests done for the data backups. You cannot have your backups and when it's time for you to use the information from those backups, they are not usable.

So, there should be regular testing of the data backups to ensure that they are usable to get you back to normal business operations within a reasonable time frame.

All this should be documented, and the results should be available so that the external auditor will be able to rely on that information.

Configuration change monitoring

Whenever configurations at the application, operating system, database or network levels have been baselined, a snapshot of such configuration should be securely stored as the "golden copy." Triggers should be implemented on the systems to alert administrators of configuration changes. All such changes should be authorized by management and documented.

Vulnerability assessment and penetration testing

While vulnerability assessment (VA) and penetration testing are generally not included in an information systems audit relating to financial reporting, it is an activity that management should consider. VA identifies weaknesses or gaps in the information systems and network layers, but these gaps have not proven to be exploitable.

VA should be done at least quarterly and validated by penetration testing which is done annually. Penetration testing validates the vulnerabilities found in the VA results that can be exploited by a threat actor if discovered.

So how do you feel now after hearing all this information?

Your next step...

Share your comments and/or feedback at https://bit.ly/3Hm6MKB

8

Unlock the Secrets

"Increase sales and reduce costs."

~Daymond John

NEW GAME-CHANGING BOOK!

SPECIAL OFFER!

Get your <u>Special Discount</u> paperback books for just $1,595 USD*

Please send 100 copies of *Think Like A Millionaire Auditor* for only $1,595*...

○ to me (new orders only).

○ as a gift, to the person named below.

○ to me and also as a gift.

☐ Cheque or money order enclosed.
(Make payable to *Harrison Cyber Security Intelligence Inc.*)

My Name _____
Please print. (Mr., Mrs., Miss, Ms.)

_____
Street

_____
Country, City, Province, Postal Code

_____
E-mail (to receive e-mail updates and special offers from Harrison Cyber Security Intelligence)

Send Gift To _____
Please print. (Mr., Mrs., Miss, Ms.)

_____
Street

_____
City, Province, Postal Code

_____
Country, Zip/Postal Code

Want 1000 copies and save even more...guaranteed? Send e-mail to info@michaelharrisonjm.com

*All pricing in United States funds. Sales tax required if delivered in Canada. Visit michaelharrisonjm.com/taxes for more information. *Special Offer Only $15.95 per book* (retail price is $24.95). We'll take care of shipping & handling as a gift to you (Canada and USA Only). Allow for 4-10 weeks for delivery. Note: *If you selected radio #3, please also include the appropriate investment amount on cheque or money order.*

Copyright (c) 2022 Harrison Cyber Security Intelligence Inc.
All rights reserved.
Printed in Canada.

MJHL1WYNQ963

www.MichaelHarrisonJM.com

Mail cheques or money orders to:

**HARRISON CYBER SECURITY INTELLIGENCE INC.
1205 GRANT AVENUE, SUITE 712
WINNIPEG, MANITOBA R3M 1Z3
CANADA**

Are You Ready!

"Mindset + Skill Set + Action Set = Your Success"

~John Assaraf

SECRET ONE

CREATE A SECURE STORAGE LOCATION

SECRET ONE: Create a secure storage location for your audit evidence

With businesses being required to perform so many audits to satisfy management and regulatory requirements, it is a good idea to have a central storage location for your audit evidence.

This location should be accessible only to authorized personnel who are assigned to submit the requested information.

If so organized, the evidence can be easily retrieved and submitted to the authorized parties requesting the information. The secure storage location can be an ideal location to allow your external auditor access to obtain their audit evidence.

The caveat is that the audit evidence must be reliably gathered in the first place to assure that all authorized parties using the evidence are comfortable with its origin.

Based on the organization's data retention policy, the audit evidence should be handled accordingly.

www.MichaelHarrisonJM.com

SECRET TWO

GENERATE YOUR USER LISTINGS

SECRET TWO: Generate your user listing from in-scope applications, operating systems and databases

Prepare your scripts or extraction procedures to gather the user listing from the in-scope applications, operating systems and databases. These can be run upon request with very minimal time committed.

Only the time period being requested needs to be changed over time.

You and your systems auditor will be happy when you take this action!

SECRET THREE

PERFORM AND DOCUMENT ACCESS RIGHTS REVIEW

SECRET THREE: *Perform and document your access rights review*

Users, i.e., information systems administrators and business users have different access rights within applications, operating systems and databases.

Therefore, on a periodic basis, the tasks that users can perform as dictated by their access rights, should be reviewed for continued access, modified access or access removal.

The review should be done by authorized personnel with intimate knowledge of those access rights. The outcome of the review should be documented and acted upon in a timely manner.

The caveat is that the authorized personnel should not review their own access rights.

SECRET FOUR

UPDATE INFORMATION SECURITY POLICY AND PASSWORD STANDARD

SECRET FOUR: *Ensure that your information security policy and password standard is up to date*

The information security policy governs the security posture of an organization and is management's high-level statements on information security.

The contents of this policy document are rarely changed, other than the dates the document was reviewed by authorized personnel.

The password standard is derived from the information security policy and outlines the parameters that must be configured on the network, applications, operating systems and databases. This standard should also be reviewed and approved by authorized personnel.

Since password testing is a point-in-time activity, you can check alignment with the password standard at the network, application, operating system and database layers.

SECRET FIVE

DOCUMENT, DOCUMENT, DOCUMENT

SECRET FIVE: *Document your applications, operating systems and databases*

Knowing the details about your applications, the operating systems that hosts them and the databases that store application data, have multiple benefits.

It should be noted that business leaders own the applications that enable the organization to generate revenue. Therefore, the name of the application owner and/or their delegate, who is a business leader, should be documented.

Applications may be hosted on a different server other than the database that stores that application data.

The type and version of the operating system such as Windows Server 2012, Red Hat Linux 7 or iSeries V7R3, should be documented.

Similarly, database versions such as Oracle 12i, Sybase ASE 15 or SQL Server 2012 should also be documented.

Microsoft Excel or database can be used to store this information and stored securely.

On a semi-annual basis or whenever there are significant infrastructure changes, an automated process could e-mail the application owners and/or delegates to update the required information.

One benefit of having all this information documented is that it can form the baseline for asset management which feeds into your business continuity process.

By the way…If you want my coaching and support to help you identify those critical assets that cause your business to run:

Your next step…

Reserve Your FREE Complimentary Spot Today at
https://calendly.com/askharrintel

But wait…there's more!

~Kevin Harrington

BONUS SECRET ONE

CAPTURE THE DATE AND TIME

BONUS SECRET ONE: Capture the date and time when your application listings were generated

It is a good idea to capture the date and time when you generate your listings i.e., user listings, program changes or data processing incidents.

Most applications store their user data within an application database separate and apart from the transactional data of the application.

Structured Query Language (SQL) *SELECT* statements can show the executed statements. The resulting number of rows should correspond exactly with the listing that is extracted to an Excel formatted document.

One should not fabricate the date on any screenshot submitted because this would erode the credibility of previous or subsequent evidence submissions.

BONUS SECRET TWO

BUILD RAPPORT WITH YOUR STAKEHOLDERS

BONUS SECRET TWO: Build rapport with your stakeholders

All authorized parties who use the information gathered from information systems to assess operating effectiveness, should be in a collaborative mode.

If the information is gathered in a reliable and accurate way, all stakeholders will be happy to not duplicate efforts of providing the same information to multiple requesters.

This is where the central storage location comes into play and all authorized parties are aware of its contents.

Interaction among all stakeholders should take place year-round to reduce the tension that may arise from the seemingly sudden requests for information at audit time.

After all, we are all human beings with a desire to be understood.

Bringing It All Together

Now, it sounds like you have discovered the core IT controls that support your financial reporting.

Take a deep breath and grab a drink of lemon water.

All the information that you need, I have given to you. Here's what you have discovered today in this book:

You have discovered the four-step UPCO blueprint:

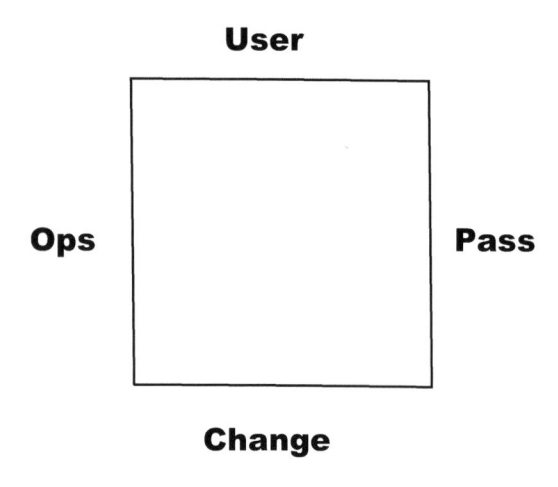

```
            User
        ┌─────────┐
    Ops │         │ Pass
        │         │
        └─────────┘
           Change
```

That's a nice little phrase that you can easily remember along with the acronym UPCO which is really, user access management, password and configuration management, change management and operations (i.e., computer operations).

So, you discovered in step 1, user access management and the several controls that are under this domain

- The granting of users
- The removal of users
- Access rights review of these users whether they are normal users or privileged users and
- The review of the activities of privileged users

In step 2 of password and configuration management, you discovered several components of the password, of the password standard that needs to be in place.

You discovered the account lockout policy and about single sign-on authentication. Also, the direct application authentication. You discovered the weaknesses of legacy applications which exist in a lot of organizations today.

You discovered the monitoring of the changes to password parameters.

In step 3, you discovered the change management process where different roles are involved in effecting a change to an application and/or system. These roles were the developer of the change, the tester of the change and the implementer of the change. You also discovered the fact that there should be segregation of duties (SoD) between these individuals.

You discovered that the developer should not be the implementer of the change into production. Also, there should be management approvals of the test results and also the changes that are going into production itself.

You discovered that in the post implementation review, there can be changes that can go undetected and not pass through the change management application.

You discovered how you can capture those changes to ensure that management has approved all the changes that have migrated into production.

Then you discovered in the step 4, computer operations, that the backups should be done according to what is configured and there should be testing of those backups to ensure that the enterprise is able to recover from any business disruptive event.

So, you have discovered our four-step blueprint Users Pass Change Ops, UPCO, that will help you reduce IT risks to financial reporting to an acceptable level and enhance your IT audit experience.

Now was our time together meaningful?

Do you feel more confident knowing about IT controls you should have in your business?

I have absolute confidence that you can take all this information that you have discovered here and on your own, go and implement this in your enterprise.

I am also certain that with the information you have now, you can with the time and effort you have, and your resources, you can go and implement this the way that most people will never be able to do.

But what if there was another option, an option that allowed us to work together?

A chance to go deeper than you have in this book.

If there was such an option for you, would you love to hear about it?

Your next step…

Ask about our **_Train the Trainer Program_** at https://bit.ly/3Hm6MKB

The Reward

Coming to Canada has been a very rewarding experience for I and my family.

I was able to work among talented people and advice decision-makers in various organizations with my expertise. I have increased in knowledge in many areas, and I want to be able to help you, so that you no longer worry about losing money in an audit.

There are four distinct seasons that I enjoy here in Canada. Spring, summer, autumn and winter. So, it is not all white snow as many would imagine. But there are four distinct seasons that are very wonderful for you to experience.

You can experience that through you being part of my universe and discover the game-changing expert advice that will allow you to thrive in your business, leadership and/or life.

ONE LAST MESSAGE

Congratulations!

I am so delighted for you making the great decision to better yourself, your leadership and your business by reading the strategies, secrets and personal stories in this book.

My mission with this book is to uplift, inspire and empower you to transform your life into one of harmony, peace and reaching your full potential.

I trust that you become inspired and empowered to LIVE WITH INTEGRITY, PEACE OF MIND and MAKING A DIFFERENCE!

Whether you are achieving your biggest dreams is solely up to you. "Success in any endeavor is the progressive realization of a worthy goal," said Earl Nightingale.

However, by following the strategies and secrets like those in this book, YOU CAN begin to gain the necessary knowledge that is required to produce your desired result.

YOU CAN DO IT because YOUR TIME IS NOW!

Again, congratulations!

"Be the hungry lion that stands up and moves to fill his hunger."
-Michael J. Harrison

ACKNOWLEDGEMENTS

Through the years, many have shared ideas, mentoring and support that have impacted my life, each in a different way. It's impossible to thank everyone and I apologize for anyone not listed. Please know that I appreciate you greatly.

First and foremost, I thank the Creator within me for all of the blessings I am fortunate to have in my life! Special gratitude must go to: James Malinchak, Nick Unsworth, Megan Unsworth, Bob Proctor, Kim Walsh Phillips, Shanda Sumpter, John Assaraf, Myron Golden, Rabbi Daniel Lapin, Lady JB Owen, Kevin Harrington, Daymond John, Jay Abraham, Tony Robbins, Peggy McColl, Price Pritchett, Brian Tracy, Les Brown, John Lee Dumas, Grant Cardone, Rachel Miller, Pete Vargas, Pat Quinn, Dean Graziosi, Jenna Kutcher, Anik Singal, Bari & Blue Baumgardner, Pedro Adao, Russell Brunson, Sonia Ricotti, Russ Ruffino, Weston Lyon, Jack Canfield, Patty Aubrey, Carolyn Bell Wisdom, Hugh Thompson, Rob Reimer, Erwin McManus, Hal Elrod, Ryan Deiss, John Ruhlin, Michael Hyatt, Jamie Kern Lima, Justin Forsett, Roger Love, Shaun T, Ray Higdon, Mary Morrissey, Dan Fleyshman, Taylor Welsh, Rory Vaden, Molly Bloom, Johnny Wimbrey, Lisa Nichols, Jesse Itzler, Ed Mylett, John C. Maxwell, Pat Flynn, Brendon Burchard, Jim Kwik, Ryan Stewman, Joel Marion, Gloria Mayfield Banks, Jeff Walker, Ray Edwards, John Jantsch, Jarrod Gandt, Dr. Myles Munroe, Craig Clemens, Ryan Levesque, Darren Hardy, Trent Shelton, Jasmine Star

*Special **FREE** Bonus Gift for You*

To help you to achieve more success, there are
FREE BONUS RESOURCES for you at:

www.FreeGiftFromCoachMichael.com

- Cutting-edge training video on how top achievers attract more career opportunities, magnetize recruiters and create more sought-after skills
- Downloadable IT audit request template called: "Get Relevant Audit Data Now"

ABOUT MICHAEL

Michael J. Harrison uses his competencies in CISSP, CISA and CRISC to empower purpose-driven clients have peace of mind about the relevant controls protecting their financial information systems. He happens to love this business of transformation and loves empowering clients who want strategic advice or insights to find roles in their life that they love as much as he does.

www.MichaelHarrisonJM.com

Michael is an international speaker, having spoken for boardroom executives, faith-based organizations, elementary schools, youth groups, associations, and business professional groups. He believes that every success, whether in business, leadership and/or life, starts with a plan and the persistence in following that plan to completion.

www.MorningSuccessPlan.com

ADDITIONAL RESOURCES

MORNING SUCCESS HOME STUDY COURSE

How to achieve your BIGGEST dreams in 4 easy steps whether in life, leadership and/or business

To order go to:
www.MorningSuccessCourse.com

*Special **FREE** Bonus Gift for You*

To help you to achieve more success, there are **FREE BONUS RESOURCES** for you at:

www.FreeGiftFromCoachMichael.com

- Cutting-edge training video on how top achievers attract more career opportunities, magnetize recruiters and create more sought-after skills
- Downloadable IT audit request template called: "Get Relevant Audit Data Now"

Manufactured by Amazon.ca
Bolton, ON